D0821522

DATE DUE

DEMCO 128-5046

Frontier Schools and Schoolteachers

Ryan P. Randolph

The Rosen Publishing Group's

PowerKids Press™

New York

To my wife, Joanne, thank you for everything

Published in 2003 by The Rosen Publishing Group, Inc.
29 East 21st Street, New York, NY 10010

Copyright © 2003 by The Rosen Publishing Group, Inc.

American Kids 2-9-04 $19.33

34322000215375

First Edition

Managing Editor: Kathy Kuhtz Campbell
Book Designer: Emily Muschinske

Photo Credits: Cover, title page, pp. 5, 6, 7 courtesy of Fred Hulstrand History in Pictures Collection NDIRS-NDSU, Fargo; back cover, pp. 9 (top left), 14 (bottom) courtesy of Northwest Museum of Arts and Culture/Eastern Washington State Historical Society, Spokane, Washington, ER7.3.7, L91-8, L97-29.89; pp. 5 (top), 6 (inset), 10 (top right), 17 (inset), 19, 20 © Nebraska State Historical Society; pp. 8, 9 (bottom), 10 (top left), 13, 17, 21 courtesy of the Denver Public Library, Western History Collection, images X-30956, X-30962, X-11858, X-30979 (top), X-6229 (bottom), X-7967, X-13558; p. 10 (bottom) courtesy of the Western History Collections, University of Oklahoma Libraries; p. 14 (top left and top center) courtesy of the Clarke Historical Society, Central Michigan University; p. 14 (top right) courtesy of the Idaho State Historical Society; p. 18 courtesy of MSCUA, University of Washington Libraries, NA4018, NA4019.

Randolph, Ryan P.
Frontier schools and schoolteachers / Ryan P. Randolph.— 1st ed.
    p. cm. — (The library of the westward expansion)
Includes bibliographical references (p.   ) and index.
ISBN 0-8239-6295-4 (lib. bdg.)
1. Rural schools—West (U.S.)—History—19th century—Juvenile literature. 2. Teachers—West (U.S.)—History—19th century—Juvenile literature. 3. Frontier and pioneer life—West (U.S.)—Juvenile literature. [1. Schools—History—19th century. 2. Education—History—19th century. 3. Frontier and pioneer life—West (U.S.)] I. Title. II. Series.
LC5147.W47 R36 2003
371.009'78'091734—dc21
                                        2001006968

Manufactured in the United States of America

Contents

A Different School

Today's schools are very different from the nineteenth-century schools that students attended on America's **frontier**. When white **pioneers** first arrived in the West, the region west of the Mississippi River, the West had no schools. As more pioneers continued to move west between 1840 and 1900, they built schools and established **standards** of education. However, it took time to set up governments and schools on the frontier. Children who lived in these frontier areas learned their lessons in a different way from the children who lived in the cities in the East. In the East, most children went to school on a regular basis and had experienced teachers instructing them. In the West, children often did not attend formal schools. Even when a one-room schoolhouse was built, the community members who hired teachers often could not find one to teach school-aged children.

Top: Many schoolhouses, such as this one in Cherry County, Nebraska, were small shacks made of boards and tar paper, a thick paper coated with hot tar. Bottom: Around 1900, students gather in front of a one-room schoolhouse that was located perhaps in North Dakota.

Below: *In the early 1900s, a family near White River, South Dakota, stands outside a sod home. Right: A family poses with a special plow, known as a grasshopper, near Broken Bow, Nebraska, in 1888. Education was second in importance to building a home and to working the land.*

Education on the Trail

While settlers traveled along the trails to the West, their children could not go to school. Some educated parents taught their children to read and to write while riding in covered wagons to their new homes. Children learned to read using the Bible, the sacred book of Christianity, which often was the only book people owned.

When a family reached its new home on the frontier, it worked hard to build a **homestead**. Establishing schools would come later. Some parents believed that sending their children to school would get in the way of important farmwork the children had to do.

Frontier families depended on children to help do important chores so that the entire family could stay alive.

DID YOU KNOW?

In the 1800s, country schoolhouses were sometimes named for animals and places. Some examples are Wyoming's Poison Spider School, Oregon's Pleasant Valley School, and Kansas's Buzzard Roost School.

Native American Learning

Above: *In this 1888 photo, Creek students at the Mission School at Muskogee Indian Territory wear western-style dress.*

Native American children learned about the ways of their tribes by playing games, by copying their parents and other adults, and by listening to stories. These stories described heroes, great battles, and the history and beliefs of the Native American nations. Through these stories, children learned how to behave and how to be brave and strong.

In the 1830s and 1840s, the U.S. government forced many Native American nations from their homelands to the Indian Territory, or today's Oklahoma. In the 1880s and 1890s, **boarding schools**, **mission schools**, and **reservation** schools were built to teach Native American children reading, writing, and arithmetic. Students learned how to blend in with the white **culture** by learning about white people's religions and language and by wearing white people's styles of clothing.

Left: Two young Native Americans wear western clothes under their traditional blankets as they sit in front of a tepee in 1899. Below: Around 1900, children eat dinner at the Supai Indian School in Cataract Canyon, Arizona. At mission and reservation schools, Native American students learned the white people's way of life at the expense of native culture and religious beliefs.

The First Schools

People living on the frontier built the first schools from whatever materials or structures they could find. Some students attended school in a wagon, a **brush arbor**, an unused **dugout**, or even a deserted cabin. After the settlers built a few houses to form a community, they usually constructed a one-room building out of logs or **sod** to serve as a schoolhouse.

A schoolhouse was not only a classroom, but also a community center. People held town meetings, dances, elections, weddings, and funerals there. These early schools had dirt floors and big iron stoves that provided heat.

Top Left: *Around 1865, a one-story, wood frame building in Boulder, Colorado, was the first schoolhouse in the state.* Top Right: *In 1891, students at the Prairie Center School in Custer County, Nebraska, were protected from winter winds by a sturdy sod building.* Bottom: *Brush arbors, such as this one built in Texas in 1887, served as classrooms in areas where the weather was warm and dry all year.*

DID YOU KNOW?

Many settlers on the frontier built sod huts, or soddies, for houses and schools. They cut blocks of sod from the ground and stacked them like bricks. They covered the walls with mud and built a roof of branches covered with sod.

Frontier Teachers

The pioneers of new settlements usually had a hard time finding teachers for their children. When a community could afford to hire a teacher, it did so on a **subscription** basis. Each family paid the teacher one or two dollars every month for each child that the family sent to school. Teachers lived in the homes of their students and received meals there, too.

Before the 1880s, teachers were not specially trained to teach. They needed only to have graduated from the eighth grade. School boards, the people who hired the teachers, found it hard to hire experienced teachers. Often they sought the teacher who would teach for the least amount of money, rather than the person who had the most experience. Until 1890, men teachers earned higher wages than did women teachers for the same work.

This Aspen, Colorado, class from around 1885 was taught by a woman, who stands at the back of the room. In these early schools, students usually sat on benches instead of at desks.

Right: *In this 1870 photo, Native American schoolboys in Iowa pose with their teacher, a white man, who stands in the center.*

Supplies and One-Room Schools

In early frontier schools, some teachers had to write lessons on the dirt floor, because there was no chalkboard. Students brought a small **slate** to write on, a pencil, and a lunch, which was usually packed in a tin pail. Before the 1860s, children went to school at the age of three or four. Children of different ages and abilities attended the same one-room school and most were taught from the same lessons. The youngest students used primers, or small books that combined reading, grammar, and spelling. Then they advanced to readers, such as the popular *McGuffey's Eclectic Readers*.

Students sit at their desks in a classroom in Fort Spokane, Washington. Top Left: My Own Primer, published in 1857, taught reading, spelling, and religious lessons. Top Middle: A spelling lesson from My Own Primer shows words in three syllables. Top Right: In 1894, second-grader Maude Fowler completed this writing exercise called Memory Gems.

DID YOU KNOW?

Readers combined lessons in reading, grammar, geography, and arithmetic. Students learned their lessons by learning them by heart, by copying them, and by reciting them, or repeating them from memory.

Going to School

Getting to school in the West between 1840 and 1900 was often a challenge. Students traveled great distances on foot, on horseback, or by wagon. Most schooling on the frontier ended at eighth grade, but high schools did exist in large towns. Children from nearby small towns often traveled long distances daily to go to high school. Others lived with townspeople during the week and traveled home on the weekend. During planting and harvesting seasons, many students stayed home to do farmwork.

There were no restrooms in one-room schools. Instead students used an **outhouse**. Even with a stove in the classroom, winters on the **prairies** could be so cold that schools often closed in December and did not open again until the spring.

In the 1870s, students traveled on foot or on horseback to schools like the Del Norte schoolhouse near Del Norte, Colorado. Inset: In this photo taken during the summer of 1887, a young girl from Custer County, Nebraska, holds her tin lunch pail. The summer term stretched from May to late August.

433

LAUNDRY.

TAILORING.

SEWING ROOM

Learning by Doing

Children played an important part in the success of the family's homestead. Often it was more important that children do their chores than go to school. Boys learned to handle horses, to plow, to plant and harvest crops, and to hunt. Girls learned to milk cows, to make candles, to sew, to cook, to wash clothes, and to take care of younger children. These roles were not always followed closely. Boys had to help wash clothes, cook, or milk cows. Girls, too, helped to plant and to harvest crops. Shopkeepers' children stocked store shelves and measured dry goods.

Left: In 1887, at the Indian Training School at Chemawa, near Salem, Oregon, young women and men learned many different tasks to use in their daily lives. Right: In 1886, a girl poses beside a homegrown pumpkin in Broken Bow, Nebraska.

DID YOU KNOW?

Students in the West spent their spare time playing games, such as hide-and-seek, checkers, kick-the-can, and snap-the-whip. Boys spent time hunting small animals or fishing. Girls sewed or played with homemade dolls.

Men and Women Teachers

Many young women worked as teachers until they married. An unmarried woman teacher, called a schoolmarm, often came from the East and had some teaching experience. Other teachers were young women who had graduated from the schools that hired them. School boards hired men teachers especially for the winter term, when 17- and 18-year-old boys, who did farmwork in the summer, could attend school. School boards thought that men teachers could control these older boys better than could the women teachers. In 1871, in Nebraska and Kansas, around half of the teachers were men. By the 1890s, with the creation of state and local school systems, most of the teachers hired were women.

Right: Teacher Elsie Thomas, seen here with her students in 1889, instructed children in a sod school near Merna, Nebraska.

Opposite page: In this 1904 photo, students at the Shawnee School in Park County, Colorado, pose with their teacher, John B. Drake, who stands at the far left. A community expected a teacher to set an example for the students and to be honest and moral.

Into Modern Times

The idea of free public education run by a state or a territory and paid for by public tax dollars became accepted by most Americans by the 1860s. The quality of education improved as lessons were made standard throughout a state. Teachers had to pass tests to be allowed to teach at public schools. In the early 1900s, to save money and to help manage school districts, state school officials began to combine country schools into large buildings. The schools had many classrooms, numerous teachers, and many students. Improved roads and the use of automobiles meant fewer students had to walk long distances to school.

There are many small country schools in existence in the United States even today, but there are very few one-room schoolhouses. The legacy of these frontier schools and schoolteachers and their strong connection to communities will never be forgotten.

Glossary

boarding schools (BOR-ding SKOOLZ) Schools where students live during the school year.

brush arbor (BRUSH AR-ber) A place that is covered and shaded by twigs or branches that have been cut or broken off from trees.

culture (KUL-chur) The beliefs, customs, art, and religions of a group of people.

dugout (DUG-owt) A shelter dug into the ground or the side of a hill.

frontier (frun-TEER) The edge of a settled country, where the wilderness begins.

homestead (HOHM-sted) The home and adjoining land occupied by a family.

mission schools (MIH-shun SKOOLZ) Schools set up by missionaries, or people sent by a religious group to spread the religion and promote goodwill in another country or region.

outhouse (OWT-hows) A small building used as a toilet and that was common in the days before people had indoor plumbing.

pioneers (py-uh-NEERZ) The first people to settle in a new area or territory.

prairies (PRAYR-eez) Large areas of flat land with grass but few or no trees.

reservation (reh-zer-VAY-shun) An area of land set aside by the government for Native Americans to live on.

slate (SLAYT) A chalkboard. A tablet of bluish gray rock on which someone writes.

sod (SOD) The top layer of soil that has grass growing on it.

standards (STAN-derdz) Rules used to set an example or serve as something to be copied; guidelines established by an authority.

subscription (sub-SKRIP-shun) An arrangement by which one agrees to receive and to pay for something.

Index

Primary Sources

Page 5 (top). *Tar Paper Schoolhouse in Cherry County, Nebraska.* This 1905 photograph is housed at the Nebraska State Historical Society. **Page 5 (bottom).** *Reading and 'Riting and 'Rithmetic: Taught by the Tune of a Hickory Stick.* This photograph from the early 1900s is part of the Fred Hultstrand History in Pictures Collection at the North Dakota State University Institute for Regional Studies. **Page 6 (bottom).** *Mr. and Mrs. David Vincent and Daughter, Martha, by Their Sod House.* This photo was taken in the 1910s near White River, South Dakota. **Page 8.** *Miss Robertson's Scholars at the Mission School at Muskogee Indian Territory.* J. F. Standiford of Parsons, Kansas, took this photo in 1888. **Page 9 (top).** *Spokane Girls Named Lizzie Hammer Quintana and Jessie Arche, Washington, 1899.* This photograph, taken by Harry J. Allyn, is held by the Eastern Washington State Historical Society. **(bottom).** *Supai Indian School, Children at Dinner, Cataract Canyon, Arizona.* This photograph was taken sometime between 1882 and 1910. It shows Havasupai children gathering around an outdoor dinner table in Cataract Canyon, which is part of the Grand Canyon in Arizona. **Page 10 (top right).** *Prairie Center Sod Schoolhouse, District #57, in Custer County, Nebraska.* Solomon D. Butcher took this photograph in 1891. **Page 10 (bottom).** *Public Schoolhouse, Teacher and Pupils, in Live Oak County, Texas, 1887.* This photograph of a brush arbor, which was taken by Brack, is part of the Western History Collections of the University of Oklahoma Libraries. **Page 13 (top).** *Attawa Indian Schoolboys at the Early Opening of the School.* This photo was taken by A. C. & E. T. Tuttle and it shows Native American students in Iowa around the year 1870. **(bottom).** *Aspen Schoolroom.* These elementary school children sit at wooden desks sometime between 1880 and 1890. Notice the cast iron stove in the center of the room and the chalkboard along the wall in the back of the room and along the side walls. **Page 14 (bottom).** *Fort Spokane Children's Classroom.* This photograph is kept at the Eastern Washington State Historical Society. **Page 14 (top left and middle).** *My Own Primer of First Lessons in Spelling and Reading.* This primer was prepared by Reverend John P. Carter and was published in 1857 by the Presbyterian Board of Publication in Philadelphia, Pennsylvania. **Page 17.** *Del Norte Schoolhouse.* A brick schoolhouse is located in the middle of a valley near the town of Del Norte, Colorado, next to a small stream in Rio Grande County. **Page 18 (left and right).** *Indian Training School.* These engravings were made in 1887 and they illustrate Native American children learning various vocational activities.

Web Sites

Due to the changing nature of Internet links, PowerKids Press has developed an online list of Web sites related to the subject of this book. This site is updated regularly. Please use this link to access the list:
www.powerkidslinks.com/lwe/frschool/